2019
HUMAN DESIGN
EVOLUTION GUIDE
Using Solar Transits to Design Your Year

KAREN PARKER

2019 HUMAN DESIGN EVOLUTION GUIDE
Using Solar Transits to Design Your Year
KAREN PARKER

Please visit QuantumAlignmentSystem.com
for more details, practitioners, and valuable resources.

@HumanDesignForEveryone   www.quantumalignmentsystem.com   @humandesignkaren

© 2018 by Karen Parker and GracePoint Matrix, LLC Publishing Division.
All rights reserved.

No part of this work may be used or reproduced, transmitted, stored, or used in any form or by any means graphic, electronic, or mechanical, including but not limited to photocopying, recording, scanning, digitizing, tapping, Web distribution, information networks or information storage, and retrieval systems, or in any manner whatsoever without prior written permission from the author. Some graphics courtesy of Vecteezy.com.

Please contact Karen@quantumalignmentsystem.com for permissions or bulk orders.

ISBN: 978-0-9976035-8-3
Printed in the United States

DEDICATION

To all of my students, Human Design Specialists, and Quantum Alignment Practitioners. Thank you for trusting me to be your teacher. Thank you for sharing the gift of Who You Truly Are with the world. I am because you are. I love you!

TABLE OF CONTENTS

Dedication	iii
Table Of Contents	iv
Introduction	v
How To Use This Book	vi
The Theme Of The Year	vii
Transits	1-162
Summary	163
About The Author	164

INTRODUCTION

This book is a weekly guide designed to give you a deliberate way to harness the energy of the Sun and the Moon to support you in creating what you want in your life.

Human Design is a collection of cross-cultural, ancient, and modern archetypes. An archetype is a pattern of thought or symbolic image that is derived from the past collective experience of humanity. The colored in or "defined" elements in your Human Design chart tell you which archetypes you are more likely to explore and learn from in this life time.

For example, let's say you have the Gate 10 defined (colored in red, black or checkered) in your chart.

People with the Gate 10 colored in have a tendency to explore the archetype of "Self Love" over the course of their lives. "Self Love" is an archetype, a potential expression that has a wide spectrum of potential manifestations. You can manifest the high experience of the Gate 10 as someone who genuinely loves and accepts yourself for who you are and someone who empowers others by being the highest expression of self-love and acceptance. Or, you can manifest the low experience of the Gate 10 and be a blaming person who feels like everything is everyone else's fault and feeling deeply that no one loves you.

Both of these expressions are two sides of the same coin. Because an archetype is a pattern of thought or symbolic image that is derived from your past experience, thoughts, beliefs, and even your genetics, it takes awareness and deliberate action to live the highest potential of our charts.

Over the course of a calendar year, the Sun moves through all 64 of the Human Design Gates. The Human Design Gates contain the energy code for 64 core human archetypes. As the sun moves through an archetype, it "lights up" that theme for everyone on the planet, creating a theme for the week.

We all deal with the weekly themes. Even if the theme doesn't impact your chart deeply, it will impact the charts of the people around you.

The gift of the solar transits is that it gives you an opportunity to work deliberately with all 64 of these core human archetypes and to consciously focus on living the highest expression of these energies in your daily life.

The solar transits also bring you creative energies that help you meet the goals you set for yourself each year.

The moon in Human Design represents the energy of what drives us. In traditional astrology, the new moon phase and the full moon phase represent bookend energies that mark the beginning and the end of a monthly creative cycle.

The new moon helps us set the intention for our goals for the month. The full moon supports us in releasing any energies, beliefs or blocks that are hindering the completion of our goals.

Lunar and solar eclipses are also astrological bookends. They mark beginnings and endings. The work we do in between can be powerful, internal, as well as external. Eclipse energy represents cycles that support you in aligning more deeply with your bigger goals in life, as well as support you in breaking free from habits and patterns that keep you from growing and expanding.

To learn more about the transits and how they affect your Human Design chart and your energy click here: www.quantumalignmentsystem.com/solar-transit-calendar

HOW TO USE THIS BOOK

The 2019 Human Design Evolution Guide is a workbook with weekly writing assignments, affirmations, and Emotional Freedom Techniques (EFT) setup phrases. If you are not a fan of journaling, feel free to contemplate the prompts in whatever way works for you. You may walk with them, meditate on them, or even discuss them with your friends.

The Emotional Freedom Techniques is a powerful energy psychology tool that has been scientifically proven to change your emotional, mental, and genetic programming to help you express your highest potential. Each week you may work with a specific EFT setup phrase to help you clear any old energies you may be carrying related to the specific archetype of the week.

(Learn more about how to use EFT here: www.quantumalignmentsystem.com/solar-transit-calendar)

You will also find exercises for each new moon, full moon, solar eclipse, and lunar eclipse complete with a writing/contemplation assignment and affirmation. You'll also be guided in working with the theme of the lunar cycles and eclipses so that you can make the most of these powerful energy cycles.

Every Human Design year gives us a 365 day creative cycle that supports us in releasing what no longer serve us, allows us to consciously increase our creative energy, and grow and evolve with the support of the stars.

May you have a prosperous and joyful 2019!

THE THEME OF THE YEAR

2019: The Year of Re-Writing the Story of Who You Truly Are and Mastering Faith

Each contains powerful energy to support us on our personal and planetary evolutionary path. Every year carries a theme that is highlighted and repeats in multiple layers in the "celestial weather", including during moon cycles and eclipse cycles.

This year has two powerful themes that play with each other in a complementary and powerful way. We are remembering Who We Truly Are and re-writing the stories we tell about ourselves. The planets are inviting us to look at places where we may be limiting ourselves and what's possible by holding on to old stories, traumas, un-forgiveness, and beliefs that are keeping us from fulfilling our personal and collective potential and purpose.

We are being supported by the planets by simultaneously learning to deepen our faith. The planets are inviting us to explore how our identity, life, and creative expression would transform if we knew that we were infinitely supported by the Universe. We are being asked to take great leaps of faith, to have more faith in ourselves, and each other and to remember to trust in the infinite, abundant nature of our creative power.

We are discerning this year, setting priorities and getting clear about what we truly want to be creating in our world. I predict you'll look back at this year as a catalytic and aligning year - a year when you remember Who You Are.

May this be a blessed and prosperous year for you and may you remember the Magnificence of your Authentic Self.

From my Heart to Yours,
Karen

JANUARY 22, 2019

HEXAGRAM 41 - IMAGINATION
The ability to craft a vision of what else is possible.
The initiating energy for inventiveness.
The capacity to trust that your daydream will become a reality.
Envisioning.

AFFIRMATION:

In the stillness I surrender to the Great Mystery of Life and the Divine. I allow Divine Inspiration to wash over me and I listen with great attention and appreciation. I trust that I receive the perfect inspiration and I simply let the inspiration flow to me. I am grateful.

WRITING ASSIGNMENT:

Please read, respond, and explain your response to each question below.
* What do you need to do deepen your connection with Source?

✸ Do you feel aligned with something bigger than yourself?

✸ Do you need to create a routine in your daily practice to stay centered and connected?

 **EFT SETUP:**

> Even though I don't know all the answers, I now choose to surrender and trust that I am being loved, supported, and nurtured by the Infinite Loving Source that is the Universe.

JANUARY 28, 2019

HEXAGRAM 19 - INTIMACY

The energy for intimacy.
The sensitivity to perceive subtle changes and shifts in emotional energy,
and the physical environment.

AFFIRMATION:

I am grateful for all that I have received. I honor my creative process and know that Divine Timing will open up the correct circumstances in the correct order to fulfill my creative desires and provide all the support and success I desire. I honor the nature of Divine Timing and trust that abundance works through me and my relationships at all times.

I know that the ending of cycles is always the beginning of the new. I honor the end of all creative cycles and anticipate the next new creative experiences awaiting me. I take the blessings and the lessons I have learned from this cycle and move forward courageously into the next.

I take great care of all my relationships, including my relationship with myself. I know that some relationships will serve me for a lifetime and some have a brief impact on my life before a new cycle begins. I begin and end all my relationships with love. I let go with ease. I allow with ease.

I trust in the cycles of Divine Order.

WRITING ASSIGNMENT:

Please read, respond, and explain your response to each question below.

* What cycles in my life are coming to an end?

* Am I resisting or allowing these conclusions?

* Is there anything I need to do to create space for the beginning of a new cycle?

* What lessons have I learned from this cycle?

* Which blessings am I taking with me into the new cycle?

* Where do I have new clarity?

* What does intimacy mean to me?

* Are my needs being met?

* Am I meeting the needs of my partner?

* Am I asking clearly for what I want?

* Am I allowing my partner to give to me?

* Are there places where I need to master fulfilling my own intimacy needs?

 **EFT SETUP:**

Even though it's scary to open my heart, I now choose to create space for deep, intimacy, and love in my life and I deeply and completely love and accept myself.

FEBRUARY 2, 2019

HEXAGRAM 13: THE LISTENER

The capacity to listen and hold the secrets and stories of others.
Through hearing and holding stories, you have the ability to find the gifts in the story and reframe the story to better serve you and others.

AFFIRMATION:

I am a servant to the Divine. In my quiet retreat, I align with my Higher Purpose and I take actions that are of service to the Greater Good.

Each day I ask that my mind, my eyes, my words, my heart, my hands, my body, my Light, and my Being be used in Divine Service. I am grateful for all that has come before me and I ask that I take the lessons from my past and use them to be of service to others.

I listen carefully to the words and true meanings of others. I allow myself to see the truth behind all words so that I always know the Divine Meaning of each communication.

I am clear. I am present. I take my time to respond meaningfully. I speak words that open doors of opportunities to others. I hold a sacred space for humanity to come together to fulfill it's Highest Purpose. I lead with love.

WRITING ASSIGNMENT:

Please read, respond, and explain your response to each question below.
- What is the status of my ego?

* Am I comfortable serving the Higher Good without recognition?

* Are there areas where I am still motivated by a need to prove something?

* What can I do to listen and truly hear others better?

* What do I need to do to hear and listen to my own guidance better?

* Am I taking the time for myself to allow for clarity?

* Do I see the Truth of my past?

* What pieces from the past do I still need to release?

 **EFT SETUP:**

> Even though I'm afraid to speak my truth, I now share the truth from my heart and trust that I am safe and I deeply and completely love and accept myself.

FEBRUARY 4, 2019

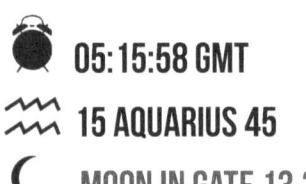

05:15:58 GMT

15 AQUARIUS 45

MOON IN GATE 13.3

The first new moon of the Human Design years sets the tone for what you're going to create this year. The entire year continues the theme from 2018. We are in a powerful global cycle that is compelling us to look at the stories we tell about who we are. The stories tell about our past, present and future, influence the direction our lives take and what we create and experience.

This new moon is about taking inventory of your story.

What stories are you telling yourself about your:
- Money
- Health
- Career/Creative Fulfillment
- Lifestyle
- Relationships
- Spiritual Connection

Take some time today and think about your ideal life.

 WRITING ASSIGNMENT:

Please read, respond, and explain your response to each question below.
- How would you like to improve the areas above?
    - Money

- Health

- Career/Creative Fulfillment

- Lifestyle

- Relationships

- Spiritual Connection

✸ What would you like your life to look like in each of these areas?

✸ During this lunar cycle I intend to:

FEBRUARY 8, 2019

HEXAGRAM 49: REVOLUTION
The ability to break relationship bonds and agreement
if the rules of the relationship aren't honored.

AFFIRMATION:

After contemplation and alignment, I now take guided actions to revolutionize my life. I am clear and I know exactly the actions to take to create lasting change and transformation in my life. I am empowered. My choice and actions are deliberate. I am ready to redefine and recreate all agreements in my life to align them with the Truth of my unlimited abundance.

My relationships are mutually respectful, loving, honoring, and for the highest good of those involved. I am clear in my communication. I set good boundaries for myself and take actions that are unconditionally loving and respectful of my partners. I only make agreements that acknowledge my beauty, my strength, my value and my worth. My agreements bring me reward in accordance with these beliefs.

I recognize that honesty and transparency and clearing acting on what is correct for me creates true intimacy and the possibility for long-term commitment. I stand fearlessly in the face love, ready to give and receive love in all of its expressions.

I embrace the changes necessary to make room for Love in my life.

WRITING ASSIGNMENT:

Please read, respond, and explain your response to each question below.
- What actions do I need to take to make room for love in my life?

- What conversations do I need to have?

- What agreements in my partnerships do I need to change?

- Are there actions that I need to take to express my love and appreciation more deeply?

- Are there places where I need to create more honoring, understanding and respect for my partners?

Revolution for Transformation
- What actions to do need to take to start a transformational revolution in my life?

* What habits, intentions, and desires need to be acted on the anchor them in form in my reality?

* More thoughts on REVOLUTION:

 **EFT SETUP:**

> Even though I'm afraid to ask for what I need, I now boldly open the space for me to receive and create the love I desire and I deeply and completely love and accept myself.

FEBRUARY 14, 2019

HEXAGRAM 30: THE CLINGING FIRE
The intensity and passion to hold a vision until it becomes manifest.

 **AFFIRMATION:**

> I am clear about my intentions and desires. I honor myself for creating the space to bring forth my dreams and intentions. My life is completely open to receive and I stand in a passionate place of anticipation for the manifestation of my desires. I only focus on what I want. My vision is true; my passion is fed by the fire of my heart. I am unwavering and powerfully focused.

WRITING ASSIGNMENT:

Please read, respond, and explain your response to each question below.
- What do I want in my life?

- What do I choose to experience in my finances, my health, my relationships, my creative fulfillment, my spiritual life, and my lifestyle?

* What distractions do I need to remove in order to keep my focus sharp?

* What am I passionate about?

* Am I free to express my passion?

* What keeps me from my passion?

 **EFT SETUP:**

>Even though my excitement feels like fear, I now choose to go forward with my passion on fire, fully trusting the infinite abundance of the Universe and I deeply and completely love and accept myself.

FEBRUARY 19, 2019

HEXAGRAM 55: ABUNDANCE
The faith to trust that you will be given all that you need
to sustain yourself and manifest your dream.

 **AFFIRMATION:**

I am aware of the Abundance of Spirit within me. I know that when I am focused on this Abundance in Spirit that all my desires are fulfilled and it is impossible for me to experience lack or need. I am completely supported and fulfilled by this awareness. By letting go and letting God, I allow abundance in all aspects of my life to manifest fully for me. Abundance is my birthright and my natural state.

 **WRITING ASSIGNMENT:**

Please read, respond, and explain your response to each question below.
* What do I need to do to release any worries and fears I may have about abundance in my life?

* What beliefs do I have about being fully supported, and abundant?

* Do I need to align these beliefs with what I know is Truth?

* What does being aware of the Abundance of Spirit within me feel like?

* What does it look like?

* How would being constantly aware of this fulfilling energy change my life?

* What do I need to do to be ready for this level of faith and trust?

 **EFT SETUP:**

Even though in the past I let fear stop me, I now choose to act as if I'm fully supported and trust in the outcome and I deeply and completely love and accept myself.

FEBRUARY 19, 2019

15:53:28 GMT

♍ 0 VIRGO 42

☾ MOON IN GATE 59.1

The full moon asks us what needs to be healed, released, aligned, and brought to your awareness for you to continue taking powerful steps in manifesting your intentions.

The Gate 59 is an energy that forces us to explore two powerful themes in our lives. Firstly, the Gate 59 is an energy that is about support and impact.

WRITING ASSIGNMENT:

Please read, respond, and explain your response to each question below.
* What do you need to release to feel more aligned with being supported and having a greater impact in your life and in the world?

Secondly, the Gate 59 is an energy that is about caring, nurturing, and sexuality.
* Are your relationships giving you support you need?

* How can you cultivate deeper intimacy and caring in your partnership?

* What do you need to release to make room for a deeper feeling of connection and alignment with your partner or your future partner?

The moon is asking you to heal your past stories about partnership, support and sexuality.
* What will you release tonight?

FEBRUARY 25, 2019

HEXAGRAM: 37 HARMONY
The ability to stabilize relationships and the energy
to find a peaceful and fair outcome.

 AFFIRMATION:

After the storm there is always calm. It is in the quietness that follows shift and change that I remember my bearings, breathe deep, and realign my relationships with what is new. All agreements I make are clear and created with peace as the end goal. From the remnants of the past, I discover the blessings and I work with my friends, my family, my tribe, my community, and my world to co-create a mutually respectful and deeply honoring peace. Peace is within me. I am peace. I breathe peace. I create peace and all is well.

 WRITING ASSIGNMENT:

Please read, respond, and explain your response to each question below.
- What areas of your life are in need of peace right now?

- How can you create a lifestyle that is more peaceful?

- ✹ Commit to five peace-enhancing activities to do for yourself today.
  -
  -
  -
  -
  -

- ✹ What new kinds of agreements do you need to make with your partners?

- ✹ Are your agreements with your partner clear?

- ✹ Do all parties in your agreements have the same expectations?

- ✹ Are there any clarifying conversations you need to have to deepen the awareness and clarity of your agreements?

Spend some time just hanging out and being peaceful with your loved ones this week!

 **EFT SETUP:**

> Even though sometimes it's hard to wait for the right time, I patiently trust that when the time is right, I'll take the right action to create harmony in my life and I deeply and completely love and accept myself.

MARCH 2, 2019

HEXAGRAM 63 - QUESTIONING
The power to use inquiry to think about new possibilities
and to test out new theories.

AFFIRMATION:

I trust myself. I trust the Divine. I trust that there is perfection in experimentation. I trust my insight and knowingness. I am discerning but not doubtful. I know that all questions have answers. I trust in the elegant solution and know that the answer will be mine in time and all is well.

WRITING ASSIGNMENT:

Please read, respond, and explain your response to each question below.
* What experiences have I had that have caused me to doubt myself?

* What experiences have I had that have shown me that my inner knowingness is correct?

* What are my gifts, my strengths, and my talents?

* Where have I demonstrated mastery and what do I need to do to release my self-doubt?

* Do I trust in Divine Order?

* Can I see that everything has a purpose?

* What mistakes have I witnessed that ultimately created a path to perfection and mastery?

* What do I need to do to forgive the mistakes?

* What do I need to do to integrate mistakes as a crucial part of mastery?

 **EFT SETUP:**

> Even though I struggle with trusting myself, I now choose to relax and know that I know. I listen to my intuition. I abandon logic and let my Higher Knowing anchor my spirit in trust and I deeply and completely love and accept myself.

MARCH 6, 2018

16:03:52 GMT
15 PISCES 47
MOON IN GATE 63.4

The Gate 63 is an initiating energy. This Gate represents the start of the Logical Circuit in the Human Design chart. It carries the energy of questioning. The Gate 63 energy causes you to want to know what else is possible. This query has the power to light up your creative juices.

The flip side of this energy is doubt, most commonly, self-doubt. When this energy plays with the New Moon, is forces us to stretch beyond what we think is possible and try something new, open ourselves up to possibility. Be prepared for self-doubt to raise it's ugly head and use this time to deepen your trust in your own inner wisdom, your intuition, and you own mastery.

Play wildly with your imagination tonight and dream about what else is possible for your life. Write, draw or color some of your new ideas here:

WRITING ASSIGNMENT:

Please read, respond, and explain your response to each question below.

* Where does self doubt show up for you?

* Where do you feel it in your body?

* How does it feel when you connect with your Inner Truth?

* Can you tell the difference?

* Keep a log of your intuitive hunches and make a note of how accurate they are.

    *

    *

    *

* During this lunar cycle I intend to:

MARCH 8, 2019

HEXAGRAM 22 - GRACE
Surrender.
Letting go and trusting that you will have all the resources
you need to give what you seek to share with the world.

AFFIRMATION:

I trust that when I let go and surrender to the Divine, I will be provided with all of the resources that I need to give service to the world. My words, my actions, and my energy transform those around me. When I stay in a state of positive expectation and trust, I am fully supported. Others look to me as a model of faith.

WRITING ASSIGNMENT:

Please read, respond, and explain your response to each question below.
* When faced with the emotional energy and drama of others what is my strategy to allow and be aware?

* What are my strategies for detaching?

- ✸ What am I here to share with the world?

- ✸ What are my gifts and blessings?

- ✸ How deeply do I trust in the abundance and support of Spirit?

- ✸ How can I deepen my trust?

- ✸ Where do I create drama?

- ✸ How do I feel about my own emotional energy?

- ✸ Do I like it or do I avoid it?

* Do I wait for clarity or do I jump in and clean up afterwards?

* More thoughts on GRACE:

 **EFT SETUP:**

Even though it's hard to trust myself, I now choose to trust myself anyway and I deeply and completely love and accept myself.

MARCH 14, 2019

HEXAGRAM 36 - EXPLORING
The energy to push beyond the limits of the current human story
in order to shift the ideas about what we think is possible.

🧡 AFFIRMATION:

> I embrace the new. I watch and wait. I trust my intuition and my strategy knowing that I make clear, intentional choices. My actions are in alignment with my intentions and my desires. I am the eye of the storm. My head is clear, my heart is aligned, and I only act for my highest good. I am immune to the appearances of my outer reality and I know that I am on my way to creating what I intend. My beliefs are unwavering and I am not swayed by outer circumstances. I trust in Divine Order

 ### WRITING ASSIGNMENT:

Please read, respond, and explain your response to each question below.
* What is your strategy for coping with unexpected events, chaos, and tragedy?

* How strong is your connection to Source?

* What do you need to do to strengthen it?

 **EFT SETUP:**

> Even though it's scary to be out of my comfort zone, I now choose to push myself into something new and more aligned with my Truth and I deeply and completely love and accept myself.

MARCH 19, 2019

HEXAGRAM 25 - ACCEPTANCE

The ability to find the spiritual blessing and connection in every aspect of life.
Healing by remembering your connection to Spirit.
Surrendering the personal self to the Higher Will.

 **AFFIRMATION:**

I am perfectly prepared to take my place in Divine Order. I know that my intentions can and will be fulfilled according to Divine Mind and I relax and trust. I know that there are greater unexpected outcomes that are for my higher good and I trust completely that all is well. I turn a blind eye to how things look and I know that the Truth will be revealed to me when I need to know. The Spirit of God within me is the Source of all my good.

 **WRITING ASSIGNMENT:**

Please read, respond, and explain your response to each question below.
* How much do you trust in Divine Order?

 **EFT SETUP:**

Even though in the past, I was afraid to follow my heart, I now choose to do what is right for me and know that I am fully supported and I deeply and completely love and accept myself.

MARCH 21, 2019

01:42:45 GMT
0 LIBRA 09
MOON IN GATE 46.1

The Gate 46 represents the energy of embodiment. In its high expression we experience vitality and express our self-love through taking care of our bodies. In its low expression we disconnect from our physical form, ignoring it, avoiding taking care of it, and hating the way we look or feel in our bodies.

This full moon asks you to ask your body what it needs and wants from you.

 WRITING ASSIGNMENT:

Please read, respond, and explain your response to each question below.
* Do you need to cultivate new health habits, acknowledge its pain or lack of vitality?

* Do you need more rest and self-care?

✹ What needs to be healed, released, aligned, and brought to your awareness for you to fully embody vitality and well-being?

✹ What will you release tonight?

MARCH 25, 2019

HEXAGRAM 17 - OPINIONS
The energy to think about possibilities and theories.
Insights.

 **AFFIRMATION:**

> I wait to offer my insights until I am asked. I am aware that what is Truth for me is not always Truth for others. Each one of us has our own unique journey and our perceptions create our understandings. I wait for the right people to ask me for my understandings. I know that when people ask, they will truly value my insights. My insights are valuable to those who seek them. In order to rule and be valued, I must first be of service. I serve the truth and wait for those who are aligned with my truth.

 **WRITING ASSIGNMENT:**

Please read, respond, and explain your response to each question below.
* What do you do with ideas and inspirations that spark your enthusiasm?

* Are you good at holding on to ideas and allowing the right people to be drawn to the "germinating" phase of your creation?

* What does the phrase "to serve" mean to you?

* Are you being of service?

* Do you need to do more service?

* Are you serving yourself as the foundation of the service you offer?

* Can you serve yourself without guilt?

 **EFT SETUP:**

>Even though I have a lot of ideas and thoughts to share, I trust that the insights that I have to offer are too important to blurt out and I wait for the right people to ask and I deeply and completely love and accept myself.

MARCH 31, 2019

HEXAGRAM 21 - MANAGEMENT

The ability to manage and allocate resources including money, information, and material goods in such a way that they are distributed fairly and sustainably.

 **AFFIRMATION:**

I control my thoughts and my actions. I release my need to control others. I trust that the Universe will provide all the serendipitous encounters and the magic necessary to create the manifestation of my desires so I can better serve the world. I use my energy to manage myself and my resources so that I have more to give. I trust that my mindset and my intentional actions will encourage the Universe to conspire with me. My inspiration is a source of inspiration for others. I lead by example.

WRITING ASSIGNMENT:

Please read, respond, and explain your response to each question below.
* What things in your life do you need to let go of control over?

* What do I need to do to allow others to express themselves and to hold a space for their freedom?

✸ What do I need to do to deepen my trust of Source?

✸ What old beliefs and fears need to be released so that I can move more deeply into Trust?

 **EFT SETUP:**

Even though in the past I felt like I had to control everything, I now surrender to Source and know that my abundance, my TRUE abundance, is available to me when I let go and let the Universe do the work and I deeply and completely love and accept myself.

APRIL 5, 2019

HEXAGRAM 51 - AWAKENING

The energy to awaken others to their own connection to Spirit. The capacity to use your own shocking experiences to deepen your spiritual understanding and your service to the world.

 **AFFIRMATION:**

I have the inner strength to deflect all outer shock. I am the manifestation of Spirit in form. I am courageous, steadfast, and open to the expansion of Spirit within me. My faith and courage inspire and initiate others. My vibration is high and I lift others up with the Truth of Spirit within me.

 **WRITING ASSIGNMENT:**

Please read, respond, and explain your response to each question below.
- What are the lessons that I have learned from shock?

- How have I transformed shock into strength?

- ✺ How has shock initiated me into the Love of Spirit?

- ✺ Where have I been "shocked" in ways that I need to transmute into the Love of Spirit?

- ✺ What trauma and drama from the shock do I need to release?

- ✺ How has the shock revealed to me a deeper truth and brought me to a greater awareness of Spirit?

- ✺ What do I need to do to move into gratitude?

 **EFT SETUP:**

> Even though things aren't turning out like I expected, I now choose to embrace the unexpected and trust that the Universe is always serving my Greater Good and I deeply and completely love and accept myself.

APRIL 5, 2019

08:50:22 GMT

15 ARIES 17

MOON IN GATE 51.1

The Gate 51 is the energy of initiation. We are designed to be deeply connected to Source as part of our life path and life direction. When we stray off the path, we often experience unexpected or even shocking events that serve to wake us up and get us back on track.

The high expression of this energy is a deepening of your capacity to surrender your personal life to something larger than yourself. It is the energy of service to the greater good and works when you surrender and also value your ego as the vehicle for service.

The low expression of the Gate 51 can be the experience of feeling destabilized and "kicked out of heaven" by unexpected events. To get the most out of this energy, you have to trust that all events in your life, "good" or "bad", are there for your higher good.

 WRITING ASSIGNMENT:

Please read, respond, and explain your response to each question below.
* Where do you need to deepen your place of service to the world?

✸ What are you here to give the world?

✸ During this lunar cycle, I intend to:

APRIL 11, 2019

HEXAGRAM 42 - COMPLETION
The energy to create order out of chaos
and to bring to completion things that need to end
in order to create room for the new and for expansion.

AFFIRMATION:

I embrace all the change that has come before and I recognize that all endings are new beginnings. I open the door for the new and re-dream what is to come. I am fully prepared to lay down the physical manifestation of the foundations of what is new and to take the actions necessary to bring what is new into form.

WRITING ASSIGNMENT:

Please read, respond, and explain your response to each question below.
* What final steps do you need to take to release the energy of this first quarter?

* What doors do you see opening?

* Closing?

* What clarity have you gained since the beginning of the year?

* How has that clarity helped you define what you truly want?

* What action steps do you need to take to bring this into form?

✋ EFT SETUP:

> Even in though in the past I hesitated to finish what I needed to finish in order to make room for something new and better, I now choose to bring things to a powerful ending and know that I am taking strong action to create space for what I truly want to create in my life and I deeply and completely love and accept myself.

APRIL 17, 2019

HEXAGRAM 3 - MUTATION
The energy to see what else is possible and to innovate with new ideas.

AFFIRMATION:

> I accept and embrace change and love what is. I trust that what I am experiencing right now in this moment is the perfect experience to support me in creating what I intend and desire. Each step of the journey is absolutely perfect right now.

WRITING ASSIGNMENT:

Please read, respond, and explain your response to each question below.
- How much do you trust the Universe?

- What do you need to release to deepen your trust?

* What Big Dreams are you ready to put into action?

* What is your first step?

* Check in with your mindset...are you prepared?

* Or do you need a mindset tune-up?

 **EFT SETUP:**

> Even though it's scary to take the first step, I now trust the Universe and my ability to be innovative and know that I stand on the cusp of the fulfillment of my Big Dreams. I deeply and completely love and accept myself.

APRIL 19, 2019

11:12:03 GMT

29 LIBRA 07

MOON IN GATE 50.3

The Gate 50 is an energy of caring and nurturing and is the place in the chart where we hold our values. The high expression of the Gate 50 is about aligning with the values you hold dear to you and walking your talk. This energy also helps you help others sustain those values in their own lives.

The low expression of the Gate 50 can be codependency, rigidity around values, and doing for others what they could be doing for themselves. With the moon lighting up this powerful energy, we are asked to evaluate our own values to make sure that we are living true to our values and whether we are also valuing our selves and our own life path enough to set good, clear and healthy boundaries.

 WRITING ASSIGNMENT:

Please read, respond, and explain your response to each question below.

* What needs to be healed, released, aligned, and brought to your awareness for you to live true to your values?

* What limits and boundaries do you need to set to stay true to yourself and your connection with source?

APRIL 22, 2019

HEXAGRAM 27 - NOURISHING

The energy to assume care, education, and responsibility for the growth of others.

 AFFIRMATION:

> I am responsible for aligning with what is. I trust that when faced with challenges, I will also know exactly what to do. I take care of myself and then others so that my energy is strong and my capacity to care is limitless and empowering.

WRITING ASSIGNMENT:

Please read, respond, and explain your response to each question below.
- What are you taking responsibility for that you need to release?

- Is guilt helping you hold on to something that you need to let go?

* Can you release the guilt?

* What small acts of compassion are you not taking because you don't think it will do any good?

* Can you give yourself permission to do it anyway?

* With the awareness that you are responsible for your own reality, is there anything about how you are creating your reality that you'd like to change?

* Do you need to take better care of yourself?

 **EFT SETUP:**

>Even though it's hard to say no, I now choose to take the actions that are correct for me. I release my guilt and I deeply and completely love and accept myself.

APRIL 28, 2019

HEXAGRAM 24 - RATIONALIZING

The ability to understand the vital and workable parts
of a big idea and to be able to share it with others.
The gift of finding the blessings in painful situations.

 **AFFIRMATION:**

> I give my attention to my progress and all that is good. I focus on what is working, what is aligning and I trust that all that is good will grow. I celebrate my successes and focus on creating more success by simply attending to that which is correct for me.

 WRITING ASSIGNMENT:

* Make a list of everything that feels good and is working in your life.
  -

  -

-

-

-

-

✹ More thoughts about RATIONALIZING:

✋ EFT SETUP:

Even though it's scary to start something new...I'm afraid I'm not ready...I now choose to courageously embrace the new and trust that everything is in Divine Order and I deeply and completely love and accept myself.

MAY 4, 2019

HEXAGRAM 2 - SUPPORT
The energy to realize and align with being fully supported
in all ways to fulfill your life purpose.
Receiving and gratitude.

AFFIRMATION:

I am always moving towards beauty. All of my challenges and struggles have given me the lessons to move me forward. My every step is perfect. My every movement moves me to growth and expansion and each moment of my journey is perfect.

WRITING ASSIGNMENT:

Please read, respond, and explain your response to each question below.
- What steps do I need to take to surrender to my destiny?

- How comfortable am I with the idea of "receiving"?

✳ Do I allow myself to be supported?

✳ Do I have clarity about my direction?

✳ What do I need to do to be clear?

 **EFT SETUP:**

>Even though I'm scared because nothing looks like I thought it would, I now choose to relax, trust, and receive the support that I am designed to receive. I know that I will be supported in expression my True Self and I deeply and completely love and accept myself.

MAY 4, 2019

🕛 **22:45:23 GMT**
♉ **14 TAURUS 11**
☾ **MOON IN GATE 2.1**

The Gate 2 is the most receptive energy in the chart. It sits at the bottom of the identity center, the center for love, direction and who you truly are. We are designed to receive all of the resources we need to fulfill our life purpose, but most of us struggle to allow ourselves to receive. We think we are not worthy or that we have to earn support.

What the chart shows us is that we are designed to be supported simply because we exist. There is no shame in receiving support.

This moon invites you to deepen your trust in your support for the universe. The moon is inviting you to explore how you can expand your willingness to receive everything you need to create your goals and dreams.

 **WRITING ASSIGNMENT:**

Please read, respond, and explain your response to each question below.
- ✸ Do you trust the universe?

- ✸ Do you value yourself enough to allow yourself to be supported?

✳ Do you regularly ask for the support you need?

✳ What can you do this lunar cycle to deepen your faith in your support?

MAY 10, 2019

HEXAGRAM 23 - EXPLANATION
The ability to take new ideas and paradigms, break them down into small pieces and explain the ideas clearly to others.

 **AFFIRMATION:**

My greatest strength is my ability to be still and wait to be asked to share the vision I hold. I stand with great confidence in my knowingness and I trust that I know and hold the intention to create dynamic change for my own good and for the greater good of the whole.

 **WRITING ASSIGNMENT:**

Please read, respond, and explain your response to each question below.
* What do you do to hold your vision?

* What part of your daily practice supports you in holding the energy of your intention?

* How does it feel to you when you don't know "how" something will manifest?

* How long do you hold your intention?

* Do you have the patience to wait for the right thing?

* Can you let go of your back up plan and trust the Divine Order?

* Are you preparing with small acts of faith that will show the Universe that you are prepared for the next step in your assignment?

* Do you have the courage to hold onto a vision, even when no one else "gets" it or understands it at the moment?

* Is it okay for you to be on your own with your intention?

✹ How do you feel about "not fitting in"?

✹ Where do you quit? Where do you hold steady?

 **EFT SETUP:**

Even though in the past I shut down my voice, I now speak my truth and offer the contribution of my unique spirit to the world and I deeply and completely love and

MAY 16, 2019

HEXAGRAM 8 - CONTRIBUTION

The ability to make a powerful contribution to the world
by being the full expression of your authentic self.
Your self-expression gives permission to others to do the same.

AFFIRMATION:

My contribution to humanity is important. I commit myself to making my contribution by expressing my authenticity to its fullest extent. The world needs me to play the role I intended to play and the greatest contribution I make is to share my Light, my Love, Myself with the world. I never hold back. I radiate. I am a crucial part of the Light of the Wholeness of Mankind.

WRITING ASSIGNMENT:

Please read, respond, and explain your response to each question below.
* If you could live an uncompromising life, what would it look like?

* Do you dream of making a contribution to the world?

* What is it?

* What do you need to do to bring it forth?

* Is there anything stopping you?

 **EFT SETUP:**

Even though I question whether I have something of value to add to the world, I now choose to courageously follow the whispers of my soul and live a life that is a powerful expression of the truth of who I am. I speak my truth. I value my contribution. I know I am precious and I deeply and completely love and accept myself.

MAY 18, 2019

🕛 21:11:14 GMT

♏ 27 SCORPIO 39

☾ MOON IN GATE 14.3

The Gate 14 is the only place in the chart where the energy for resources, money usually, is paired with the energy for working and the Sacral center. It's ironic though because the Sacral center can only work effectively in response to life.

In other words, the right opportunities to make money come to us when we wait and allow things to show up in alignment with right timing and cosmic order. This full moon invites you to deepen your trust in divine timing and the infinite abundance of the universe.

 WRITING ASSIGNMENT:

Please read, respond, and explain your response to each question below.
* What needs to be healed, released, aligned, and brought to your awareness for you to deepen your trust in right timing, the infinite abundance of the universe, and your ability to receive support?

MAY 21, 2019

HEXAGRAM 20 - ANTICIPATION

The energy to be aware and ready to take action when the time is right.
The awareness to know what skills and talents others have and
to be able to bring the right people together to create conscious community.

 **AFFIRMATION:**

(This week's affirmation is more of a mantra...enjoy!)
Just because I can do it, doesn't mean that I have to or that I should. I use my strategy to determine my actions and I only do the things which are correct for me. I am a door to cosmic perfection and the entrance point for actions that create Divine Order. It is in my "not doing" that my doing becomes evident.

 WRITING ASSIGNMENT:

Please read, respond, and explain your response to each question below.
* How do you feel about "not doing"?

* Are there places in your life where you are busy without direction?

* Are you battling burn-out?

* Are you being as effective as you'd like to be?

* Are there places in your life where you need to take leadership?

* Delegate?

* Define your personal power. Are you fully activating it?

EFT SETUP:

Even though it's scary to not "do" anything and wait, I now choose to trust the infinite abundance of the Universe and I deeply and completely love and accept myself.

MAY 27, 2019

HEXAGRAM 16 - ENTHUSIASM
The willingness to dive in and experiment with an idea.
Versatility.

AFFIRMATION:

I allow myself to create and experiment. Experimentation and exploration are a natural part of my creative self and allows me to find the correct pattern for the expression of my talents and my soul's journey. It is in the relentless pursuit of this journey that I live my joy.

WRITING ASSIGNMENT:

Please read, respond, and explain your response to each question below.
- What dreams are beginning to come to fruition?

- What is your experimentation teaching you?

* What are you needing to tweak?

* What beliefs may be part of creating the manifestation of your experiments?

* Are there any old beliefs that you need to release?

* Can you imagine the full enthusiastic expression of your unique gifts and talents?

 **EFT SETUP:**

Even though I'm afraid that I'm not fulfilling my life purpose and I'm wasting my life, I now choose to relax and know that I am in the perfect place at the perfect time to fulfill my destiny and I deeply and completely love and accept myself.

JUNE 2, 2019

HEXAGRAM 35 - PROGRESS

The wisdom to hold back, watch and wait.
The ability to choose deliberately, based on your own experiences and knowledge,
whether to put your energy into something or not.

AFFIRMATION:

I choose the kinds of experiences I desire. My feelings about my experiences show me what is correct for me. I am responsible for my own choices and my own happiness and no one create experiences for me that I do not choose.

WRITING ASSIGNMENT:

Please read, respond, and explain your response to each question below.
* What is going on in your life right now that you would like to change?

* In your current manifestations, what experiences would you like to avoid duplicating?

✸ How can that understanding help you get clear about your creation?

✸ What experiences do you need to focus and align with?

✋ EFT SETUP:

> Even though in the past I struggled to stay focused and move forward, I now trust myself to take the next steps on manifesting my dream. I am focused, clear and moving forward and I deeply and completely love and accept myself.

JUNE 3, 2019

 10:01:50 GMT
♊ 12 GEMINI 34
☾ MOON IN GATE 35.2

The Gate 35 is the energy of experience. From our life's adventures, we gain wisdom and understanding. We can use and share with wisdom when we discern that the energy and the timing are right for sharing.

In the low expression, this energy causes us to hold back, to feel jaded and unwilling to waste energy on something frivolous.

In the high expression, we seek to share what we know in a mature and transformative way with others.

 WRITING ASSIGNMENT:

Please read, respond, and explain your response to each question below.
* What is your wisdom? What gifts and knowledge do you have to share with the world.

* Where do you have experience?

* How can you deepen your appreciation for what you've survived and what you've learned?

JUNE 8, 2019

HEXAGRAM 45 - GATHERING TOGETHER

The energy for natural leadership.
The capacity to share your resources with others for the greater good of the whole.
Teaching energy.

 **AFFIRMATION:**

I gather to me all the people necessary to support my manifestation in my life. I take leadership and honor my role as the King/Queen of my creation. I delegate, assert my power, manage resources effectively, and act with benevolence.

 **WRITING ASSIGNMENT:**

Please read, respond, and explain your response to each question below.
* Where in my life do I need to assume a leadership role?

* How do I feel as a leader?

- Is it okay for me to be in charge, honor my creation, and speak my truth?

- What do I need to do to attract the right people into my life to serve my manifestation and creation?

- Is my mindset aligned with being a "team player"?

- Or a King/Queen?

- The shadow side of the King/Queen is over-controlling and punitive. Are there places where I need to let go of my creation and allow it to evolve?

 **EFT SETUP:**

Even though I'm afraid to look at my finances, I now choose to take a real look at my financial numbers and know that awareness is the first step to increasing my financial status and I deeply and completely love and accept myself.

JUNE 14, 2019

HEXAGRAM 12 - THE CHANNEL

The ability to articulate creative and transformative ideas when the timing and the energy is aligned.
A natural connection with Source who often serves as a vehicle for Divine Wisdom.

AFFIRMATION:

In my expression of my intention, I stay open to the Voice and Words of the Divine. My words, my expression, and my creation are Divinely Guided and I speak the perfect words to transmit the beauty of who I am and what I create. My voice is heard and valued and I continue to share my insights and my experiences as part of my creative process. My Divine perspective supports me in evolving my ideas and creations.

WRITING ASSIGNMENT:

Please read, respond, and explain your response to each question below.

* Are you using will power or Divine Power to create?

* Do you feel stuck or at a standstill?

✸ If so, what do you need to do to keep moving forward?

✸ Is it time to continue sharing your thoughts, ideas, and Divine Inspirations with others?

✸ What playful things can you do to inspire your creative energy?

 **EFT SETUP:**

> Even though I'm afraid that I'm failing my life purpose and mission, I now choose to know that I am in the right place fulfilling my right purpose and that all I need to do is to follow my strategy, be deliberate, and follow my heart and all will be exactly as it needs to be and I deeply and completely love and accept myself.

JUNE 17, 2019

- 08:30:33 GMT
- 25 SAGITTARIUS 53
- MOON IN GATE 11

The Gate 11 is the gate of ideas, opening to possibilities, and expanding the story of who we are. This is a powerful creative energy.

In its high expression, the Gate 11 assigns us the job of sacred steward for ideas. I tell my clients with the energy to keep a written log of all their ideas and hold on to them until you either experience the right timing to implement them or you meet the right person to share them with. Not all of your ideas are yours to complete, only yours to nurture and take care of and share when necessary.

The low expression of the Gate 11 is the experience of feeling confused or overwhelmed by too many ideas.

This full moon asks us what needs to be healed, released, aligned, and brought to our awareness to deepen your focus on your goals and intentions.

 WRITING ASSIGNMENT:

Please read, respond, and explain your response to each question below.
- ✵ Where are you distracted?

- ✵ What ideas do you need to put aside to stay true to your intention?

JUNE 20, 2019

HEXAGRAM 15 - COMPASSION
Lover of humanity and nature.
A deep desire to give to the world and an extreme force of nature.
Not designed to be consistent.
Is happiest when following the flow of natural order and
when finding the place where it serves the greatest need.

 **AFFIRMATION:**

My life adds to the greatness of humanity. My work benefits the world. I accept unconditionally the broad spectrum of diversity and rhythm that makes up humanity and I surrender to the larger flow of life. I am awed by the magnificence of mankind and my awe inspires me to be of service to the greater good.

 **WRITING ASSIGNMENT:**

Please read, respond, and explain your response to each question below.
* What contributions are you making to humanity?

* Are you acknowledging your service?

* Do you need or want to deepen your commitment?

* What role does rhythm play in your life?

* Does your personal rhythm bring you joy?

* Enhance your creations?

* Fulfill your intentions?

* Do you need to experiment or change your rhythm?

 **EFT SETUP:**

> Even though I feel powerless to make a difference in the world, I now choose to follow my heart and my passion knowing that I am the greatest gift I can give the world and the more I show up as my true self, the more I empower others to do the same and I deeply and completely love and accept myself.

JUNE 26, 2019

HEXAGRAM 52 - KEEPING STILL (BIG MOUNTAIN)
The ability to see the "big" picture and to have a holistic viewpoint.

♥ AFFIRMATION:

The stillness of my concentration allows patterns and order to be revealed to me. My understanding of this order gives me the power to continue to create effectively. The stillness of my concentration is the source of my power this week.

WRITING ASSIGNMENT: (IT'S A TWEAK WEEK!)

Please read, respond, and explain your response to each question below.
* What do you need to do to create stillness this week?

* In the stillness, what questions do you have?

* What patterns are being revealed to you?

✵   How deeply do you feel the alignment of Divine Order?

✵   Define your power:

✵   Where are you powerful?

✵   Do you need to amplify your power, if so, how?

✵   Do you feel good being powerful?

✵   If not, why and what stops you from your power?

 **EFT SETUP:**

Even though it makes me nervous to stop "doing" and sit with the stillness, I now trust the process and know that my state of alignment and clarity with my intentions is the most powerful thing I can do to create effectively and powerfully in my life. I relax, I trust, and let my abundance unfold and I deeply and completely love and accept myself.

JULY 2, 2019

HEXAGRAM 39 - PROVOCATION
The energy to tease, challenge and bring attention
to things that are out of alignment with abundance.
Activist.

 **AFFIRMATION:**

I wait for the right spirit of things before I progress forward. I take my time and allow the right doors to open to pathways that place me in the right place at the right time doing the right thing.

 **WRITING ASSIGNMENT:**

Please read, respond, and explain your response to each question below.
* Describe a memory when the "spirit" felt right and a correct manifestation followed.

Reconnect with that feeling and anchor deep within your body and your consciousness.

* Do you push people and opportunities away?

- Is it correct for you?

- Do you need to find more constructive ways to allow yourself more time to make decisions?

- What can you do to create an energy that is "allowing"?

- What is your relationship with food like?

- Are you an emotional eater?

- Do you love your body?

- Are there changes you need to make in your relationship with food and your eating lifestyle?

✋ EFT SETUP:

> Even though I worry about money, having the right relationship, and creating abundance in every area of my life, I now trust Spirit and allow the abundant nature of the Universe to reveal itself to me. I stay open to the possibilities of miracles and trust that all I have to do is stay conscious of the abundance of Spirit unfolding within me and I deeply and completely love and accept myself.

JULY 2, 2019

 19:16:06 GMT
 10 CANCER 38
 SUN IN GATE 39.1
 EARTH IN GATE 38.1
 MOON IN GATE 39.2

Eclipses are always bookends of energy that give us a mini cycle filled with potential for growth and expansion. Eclipses come in pairs. This eclipse marks the first member of this year's pair, setting us up to do important work redefining the story of who we truly are. The Gate 39 is the energy of provocation. As eclipses rev us up and amplify the themes we are working with, this solar eclipse cycle promises to be a doozy. The Gate 39 provokes us and shows us where we are out of energetic alignment with trust and faith. It points to the Gate 55, the energy of abundant flow in the chart.

If you are operating with any sense of lack in your life and in your creativity, it will certainly rise up for clearing during the cycle.

The purpose of this energy is to support us in explaining where we may perceive ourselves or our life as it being lacking in some way. You may feel provoked or challenged by people who reflect back to you that you feel that you're not enough or aren't worthy of having support and abundance.

This is a valuable time to work on your self worth and the value of your own contribution to the world. This energy can be deeply emotional and pressure-filled, to be sure,

Really take care of yourself during the cycle. Go for walks, sleep well, rest, meditate, spend time near water to help you release any emotional energy that might get triggered for you.

 **WRITING ASSIGNMENT:**

Please read, respond, and explain your response to each question below.
- What needs to be healed, released, aligned, and brought to your awareness for you to fully experience the infinite support and flow of abundance in your life?

JULY 8, 2019

HEXAGRAM 53 - DEVELOPMENT
The energy to start (not necessarily finish) things.
The energy for expansion.

 AFFIRMATION:

> I wait and start things according to my strategy. I allow for the energy of new beginnings and trust that when I live my strategy, all the key pieces to complete my creative process will magically align.

 WRITING ASSIGNMENT:

* Stay tuned this week to the energy of new beginnings and starting things. Allow the ideas, revelations, inspirations, and spurts of initiation energy to rev up your engines but wait according to your strategy to jump in! Make a list of your new ideas or your renewed inspirations.

    •

    •

-

-

-

-

✋ EFT SETUP:

Even though I'm scared to believe that my big dreams could come true, I now choose to trust the infinite power of the Universe and know that I am never given a dream that can't be fulfilled.

JULY 13, 2019

HEXAGRAM 62 - PLANNING
The awareness to know what might be needed
to make an experience safe, valuable, and worthwhile.
Practical and organized.

 **AFFIRMATION:**

> I use my words carefully. My words generate form for my dreams and ideas. My thoughts are clear and organized and I find and speak the truth with courage and consistency.

 **WRITING ASSIGNMENT:**

* Time for tweaking again! We're almost half way through the year. Time to revisit our vision and renew our commitment in words to our dreams. Take time this week to write out your dream in words. It is the power of our words that create things.

✴ More thoughts about PLANNING:

 **EFT SETUP:**

Even though I feel pressure to do something, I now choose to relax and trust the power of my dreams to call the right circumstance to me and I deeply and completely love and accept myself.

July 17, 2019

21:38:06 GMT
24 CAPRICORN 04
SUN IN GATE 62.4
EARTH IN GATE 61.4
MOON IN GATE 61.4

This eclipse is the first of two eclipses in this lunar eclipse cycle. It marks the entrance point to a cycle that invites us to explore possibilities beyond what we think are "reasonable" and it encourages us to maintain a state or innocence, wonder, and awe as key energies that support, not only our creative expression but our ability to feel connected to our unique place in the cosmic plan.

The gate 61 is one of the gates that connects us directly to the quantum field, the infinite source of possibilities. It causes us to ask the question "why?". Of course, the question "why" is the unanswerable question that trigger our imaginative power of dreaming up the answer. This flow state of creative dreaming "seeds" the quantum field and helps us manifest new possibilities.

When we play with this energy, we are encouraged and invited into exploring the mystery of Life, to accept what we can't change or understand, but to instead embrace the question.

We are also invited to explore where we might be rationalizing or allowing less than what we really deserve. This cycle continues to support us in deepening our faith in the infinite and abundant nature of the universe, and to discover the magic and wonder of serendipity, synchronicity, and unlimited support.

 **WRITING ASSIGNMENT:**

Please read, respond, and explain your response to each question below.
* What needs to be healed, released, aligned, and brought to my awareness for me to trust that my life purpose and soul's journey is aligning me with exactly what I need to do next, and the perfect unfolding of my life?

* What do I need to do to feel more connected to source?

July 19, 2019

HEXAGRAM 56 - THE WANDERER

The creative ability to share new ideas and information in story form.
Can share information well using allegory, simile, and metaphors.
Teaching energy.
Natural storyteller.

AFFIRMATION:

I share my ideas and my sacred stories when I am asked. I wait to share my ideas and stories with the right people who honor my inspiration and experience. Stories are the vehicle to growing the tapestry of humanity. My story is an important part of the human experience and I honor my experience by waiting for the right circumstances. My words and my dreams are valuable.

 ### WRITING ASSIGNMENT:

* Continue tweaking this week but this week really let your imagination, dreaminess, and playful expression show you all the possibilities of how your dreams may manifest. Allow yourself to stay open to limitless possibilities. Take time this week to write out the possibilities of your dream in words.

✴ More thoughts on THE WANDERER:

 **EFT SETUP:**

Even though I'm afraid to share my ideas, I now choose to take leadership with my inspirations and share my precious ideas with others and I deeply and completely love and accept myself.

JULY 25, 2019

HEXAGRAM 31 - INFLUENCE
The ability to influence leadership
and to be in tune with the needs of the people being led.
Humble leadership/service.

 **AFFIRMATION:**

> I assume my position of natural leadership when I am asked or invited to assume influence. My words, my thoughts, my ideas, and my dream are important and worthy of sharing with the right people.

 WRITING ASSIGNMENT:

* No writing this week. Meditate on True Power and Influence and what that means to you. Notice where you feel power in your body and practice connecting with this physical magnetic feeling at least once a day.

EFT SETUP:

> Even though I'm afraid to be seen, I now choose to express myself and the magnificence that is me with gusto, courage, and awareness of my own power and preciousness and I deeply and completely love and accept myself.

JULY 31, 2019

HEXAGRAM 33 - RETREAT

The ability to synthesize, through understanding
the past, many stories and experiences in order to share the narrative of humanity.
The record keeper.

AFFIRMATION:

I continue my journey inward, working with the cycles of creation and repose. My focus now is on myself, my journey, my past, and the evolution of my future. I relax and trust that what is hidden will be revealed, truth will be demonstrated and my greatest power is in Divine Timing. I trust. I wait. I know. I grow.

WRITING ASSIGNMENT:

Please read, respond, and explain your response to each question below.
- If you have not seen the results in forward momentum in your life that you have intended for this year, what do you think is holding you back?

- What story line are you living?

✸ Write the story of your limitation or label.

✸ Re-write that story as if it weren't true for you anymore.

✸ What would change?

✸ What would be different?

✸ What would the end results be?

 **EFT SETUP:**

Even though my stories from my past have held me back, I now choose to rewrite the story of my life and tell it the way I choose, with forgiveness, embracing the gifts, and honoring my courage and strength in my story and I deeply and completely love and accept myself.

AUGUST 1, 2019

 03:11:48 GMT

 8 LEO 37

 MOON IN GATE 33.2

The gate 33 is the energy of retreat. When we explore this energy, we are invited to take a step back and look at all of the places where we hold un-forgiveness and stories that take us away from the truth of who we are. We are also encouraged to literally take time to nourish, replenish, and re-Source our spirit so that we are creating in the world from a fresh and energized state.

This new moon wants you to take a pause and explore what you need to do to take care of yourself.

 WRITING ASSIGNMENT:

Please read, respond, and explain your response to each question below.
* What need rituals, routines, and habits do you need to establish to take good care of yourself?

* How would your life look if you made yourself a priority?

* How would better self-care affect your ability to complete your goals?

* Is there anyone in your life who you are holding a grudge against or unforgiveness toward?

* Write them a letter and thank them for what they taught you and acknowledge yourself for your strength and courage. Mail it if it feels appropriate. If not, burn it in a fire under the new moon.

AUGUST 6, 2019

HEXAGRAM 7 - LEADERSHIP SUPPORT
The natural ability to support a leader
in fulfilling their role to better serve the people they are leading.
"Chief of staff".

 AFFIRMATION:

I take leadership in my own life and know that I will be called out to share my influence with the world. I am empowered and I trust the geometry of the Universe to take me to exactly where I need to go to impress my authentic expression on the face of the world.

 WRITING ASSIGNMENT:

Please read, respond, and explain your response to each question below.
* Where do you need to take action and leadership in your life?

* What do you need to do to lead your dream?

* What kind of influence and recognition would you like to be experiencing in your life?

* What has kept you from recognition in the past?

* Is there anything you need to change to increase your light?

 **EFT SETUP:**

Even though I feel confused and conflicted about what to do, I trust the Divine Flow and let the Universe show me the right thing to do in the right time and I deeply and completely love, trust and accept myself.

AUGUST 12, 2019

HEXAGRAM 4 - THE ANSWER
The ability to hypothesize an answer to a question.
A drive to figure things out.

 **AFFIRMATION:**

The culmination of my thoughts and experiences grant me knowledge about how I need to proceed confidently and faithfully into the future.

 **WRITING ASSIGNMENT:**

Please read, respond, and explain your response to each question below.
- What are the next steps I need to take in my creative processes?

- What new awarenesses, knowledge, and insights do I have as a result of my thoughts, experiences, and meditations?

✋ **EFT SETUP:**

Even though I don't know what to do, I allow my questions to seed the Universe and I trust and wait with great patience that the answers will be revealed to me and I deeply and completely love and accept myself.

AUGUST 15, 2019

12:29:08 GMT

22 AQUARIUS 24

MOON IN GATE 49.4

This moon packs a very powerful punch. The Gate 49 is the Gate of Revolution. It gives us the energy to take a stand and remove anything that is not aligned with our values. Over the course of this year we've been working hard to really clarify who we are, the stories we tell ourselves about our life and what we need to do to fulfill our potential.

This full moon invites you to start a true revolution in your life, to release and take action on removing and limiting aspects of your life and to dramatically realign every aspect of your life with your values.

 WRITING ASSIGNMENT:

Please read, respond, and explain your response to each question below.
* What needs to be healed, released, aligned and brought to your awareness for you to align yourself with your right work, your right finances, your right relationships, your right health, your right lifestyle and your right alignment with source?

AUGUST 18, 2019

HEXAGRAM 29 - COMMITMENT
The energy for devotion and endurance that can lead to an unusual level of success.

AFFIRMATION:

As I prepare myself to emerge from my creative cocoon, I carefully examine my actions and make sure that my commitments are in alignment with my intentions. I only say "YES" to the things I know will bring me closer to fulfilling my dreams and I enter into my commitments according to my Human Design Strategy.

WRITING ASSIGNMENT:

Please read, respond, and explain your response to each question below.
- What are you committed to?

- What actions do you need to take to reflect and deepen that commitment?

EFT SETUP:

Even though I'm afraid to invest all my effort into my dream…what if it fails…what if I'm crazy…what if I just need to buckle down and be "normal"…I now choose to do it anyway and I deeply and completely love and accept myself.

AUGUST 24, 2019

HEXAGRAM 59 - INTIMACY
The ability to disperse ideas and energy
and to work to create resources to help sustain and nurture others.

 **AFFIRMATION:**

I radiate my desires into the Universe and impregnate the ethers with my dreams. My intentions influence the right people, the right places, the right circumstances, and the right opportunities at the perfect time and I know that I am radiating pure joyful intention all the time.

 WRITING ASSIGNMENT:

Please read, respond, and explain your response to each question below.
* Meditate (and journal) this week on what avenues of impact would best serve you, your intentions and your business.

* What is the next step in creating your intentions and your dreams.

* Where do you need to "get to work" to be ready for things to manifest?

 **EFT SETUP:**

> Even though I struggle to share my intentions, I now choose to boldly state my intentions and wait for the pieces of my creation to magically fall into place and I deeply and completely love and accept myself.

AUGUST 29, 2019

HEXAGRAM 40 - DELIVERANCE
The energy to use alone time to re-source, re-new,
and to integrate in order to re-emerge into the world,
when needed, to give new ideas and create community with others.

AFFIRMATION:

I relax in my knowingness that I am lovable and capable of allowing all the helping hands I need to make my dreams a reality. I seek out others and connect with an open heart and pure joy and love.

WRITING ASSIGNMENT:

Please read, respond, and explain your response to each question below.
- What is the nature of your relationships?

- Do you feel lonely?

* Do your relationships feel balanced?

* Do you need to go out and make more connections with others?

* Network?

* Join social groups?

* Are you connecting with the Family of Man?

 **EFT SETUP:**

    Even though it's hard to let go of relationships obligations, I now choose to release all relationships that are draining and unsupportive and I deeply and completely love and accept myself.

AUGUST 30, 2019

- 10:37:01 GMT
- ♍ 6 VIRGO 47
- ☾ MOON IN GATE 40.2

Reminder: We are still sitting on the middle of two powerful eclipse cycles, both of them pushing on us to reach deeper into our faith in the universe and to realign with our natural state of abundance.

Whenever we are pushed in these areas we have to trust in Divine Timing, not easy to do for many of us. It's tempting to try to override Divine Timing with our own personal will, but to do so can be deeply depleting and exhausting. This new moon reminds up that we are worthy of self-care and respite. When we pause and rest we become more, not less. We are capable of more, not less. We receive more, not less.

You can't afford to not re-Source yourself.

 WRITING ASSIGNMENT:

List ten things you will do to nurture yourself for the next four weeks.

1.

2.

3.

4.

5.

6.

7.

8.

9.

10.

SEPTEMBER 4, 2019

HEXAGRAM 64 - THE BIG IDEA
The tendency to get inspired by a giant idea in one big "download".

 **AFFIRMATION:**

I pay attention to inspiration and know that, when I wait with curious anticipation to see how my inspiration manifests. I am delighted and curious to see what the Universe brings.

WRITING ASSIGNMENT:

Please read, respond, and explain your response to each question below.
* What are your big dreams?

* Do you trust that they will manifest?

- What strategies do you have to stay in joy while you wait for your manifestation?

- Spend some time away from human information sources. Go for a walk or a hike in nature. Let the world give you the answers. Don't stress your brain trying to figure things out.

 **EFT SETUP:**

Even though I don't know what's next, I wait and trust that the perfect right step will show up for me and I deeply and completely love and accept myself.

Even though I feel overwhelmed with ideas, I trust the Universe to reveal the next step to me. I relax and wait and I deeply and completely love and accept myself.

SEPTEMBER 10, 2019

GATE 47 - EPIPHANY
The energy to receive the information about "how" to implement an idea.
Can't be forced.
You have to wait for the instructions and answers to reveal themselves.

AFFIRMATION:

I wait with delighted anticipation and curiosity with the expectation that the Universe manifests my desires. I keep my mindset joyful and positive and I only focus on the end result.

WRITING ASSIGNMENT:

Please read, respond, and explain your response to each question below.
* What things will you do while you are waiting for your manifestation?

* What will you do to keep your vibration high while you wait?

✸ What is the status of your mindset?

✸ Do you need to take care of your thought patterns?

 **EFT SETUP:**

Even though it's frustrating to not know how to make something happen, I now choose to wait for Divine Insight and I trust that the right information will be revealed to me at the perfect time and I deeply and completely love and accept myself.

SEPTEMBER 14, 2019

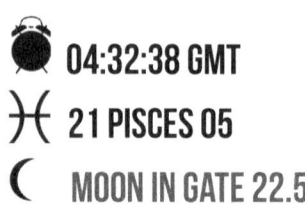

04:32:38 GMT
♓ 21 PISCES 05
☾ MOON IN GATE 22.5

The Gate 22 is the energy of grace. It's not only physical grace but also the grace that comes when we surrender and allow for divine timing and the unfolding of the cosmic plan. We can calibrate our own state of grace. Our emotions carry a frequency of energy that programs our energy field to receive and notice experiences and opportunities that match our emotions. Holding a high quality of emotional energy makes it easier for us to experience serendipity and grace.

We always have the choice to fight and struggle or to surrender with grace, to trust that we will be given everything we need to make our unique contribution to the world.

 ## WRITING ASSIGNMENT:

Please read, respond, and explain your response to each question below.
* What needs to be healed, released, aligned, and brought to my awareness for you to surrender your struggle and embrace all of the support around you?

* What do you need to do to calibrate your emotions to a state of grace?

SEPTEMBER 16, 2019

HEXAGRAM 6 - EMOTIONAL BALANCE
The energy for diplomacy and the capacity to craft peace or fight for what's right.

 AFFIRMATION:

I surrender myself to life. I trust that when I wait, the elegant solution to the challenges I perceive will reveal themselves to me. I listen with my heart and wait until I am emotionally clear before I act.

WRITING ASSIGNMENT:

Please read, respond, and explain your response to each question below.
- Are there situations in your life right now that require you to wait in order for you to craft a peaceful and loving solution?

- What do you need to do to bring out the highest expression of love, intimacy, and peace in this situation?

EFT SETUP:

Even though I'm ready to leap into action, I now choose to take a breath, wait out my emotions, and trust that the right timing will be revealed to me. I'm not missing out on anything. Divine Order is the rule of the day and I deeply and completely love and accept myself.

SEPTEMBER 22, 2019

HEXAGRAM 46 - EMBODIMENT
The recognition that the body is the vehicle for the soul
and the ability to experience and express the full vitality of Spirit in form.

 **AFFIRMATION:**

> Physical reality is an expression of my consciousness. I look to my reality to mirror my mindset and my beliefs back to me. I am clear, conscious, and awake. I am aware that I can adjust my mindset to create any physical experience I choose. I take guided actions that are in alignment with my beliefs and I celebrate this gift of being alive in a physical body!

 **WRITING ASSIGNMENT:**

Please read, respond, and explain your response to each question below.
* What is my reality telling me?

* Are there messages I need to heed?

- ✳ What discourages me?

- ✳ Do I push or do I allow?

- ✳ What do I need to do to "allow" rather than "think" my way through something?

- ✳ Are my intentions and actions an accurate reflection of my True Hearts Desires?

 **EFT SETUP:**

Even though it's hard for me to love my body, I now choose to embrace my amazing physical form and honor it for all the good it brings me and I deeply and completely love and accept myself.

SEPTEMBER 27, 2019

HEXAGRAM 18 - IMPROVING

The drive to continue to practice, correct, and repeat
in the name of becoming masterful and experiencing the joy of perfecting.
The natural ability to see patterns in others that need
to be improved in order to create more joy.

AFFIRMATION:

My entire life is a process of ever-expanding perfection. Where I am right now is the sum total of all of my experiences and as I learn and grow, so does my understanding and consciousness. I am perfect right now. My so-called mistakes are catalysts for my growth and I enjoy correcting patterns and bringing more and more alignment with my Divinity into my life! Each and every day offers me opportunities to grow and expand and I am grateful!

WRITING ASSIGNMENT:

Please read, respond, and explain your response to each question below.
* What do you need to work on releasing?

* Where in your life do you need to release judgement??

* What experiences, past or present, do you need to release and forgive?

* When you look at your life, what patterns of success and/or self-sabotage are you aware of?

* What patterns keep repeating?

* What can you do to shift these patterns?

* In your creative process, what needs to be tweaked in order to be brought into a more aligned expression?

 **EFT SETUP:**

> Even though I feel criticized and judged, I now choose to hear the wisdom of the correction and release my personal attachment and I deeply and completely love and accept myself.

SEPTEMBER 28, 2019

 18:26:14 GMT
 5 LIBRA 20
 MOON IN GATE 18.2

The Gate 18 is the energy to align patterns to create more joy. The Gate 18 is the energy to correct patterns that keep us from experiencing joy. This is an important energy that, in its high expression, helps us reevaluate everything that we're doing and explore ways to do it better. In its low expression this energy can feel critical and harsh.

Be mindful during this cycle to not be too critical of yourself and others and to not take criticism personally.

 WRITING ASSIGNMENT:

Please read, respond, and explain your response to each question below.
* What patterns and habits do you have that need to be changed or improved?

* What do you need to do to stay confident in the face of criticism?

* What needs to change in your life to help you experience greater joy?

OCTOBER 3, 2019

HEXAGRAM 48 - DEPTH
The drive to study, learn, and practice in order to become masterful.
The thirst for knowledge.

 **AFFIRMATION:**

> I trust that the skills I need will be expressed through me when I am ready. I study. I learn. I know that my knowledge will be beautifully expressed when the time and the circumstances are correct. I trust Divine Order.

 **WRITING ASSIGNMENT:**

Please read, respond, and explain your response to each question below.
* What information do you need to deepen your knowledge base?

* What do you need to learn?

✸ Do you have the skills necessary to bring forth what you desire?

✸ If not, what do you need to master?

 **EFT SETUP:**

Even though I'm afraid I'm not ready to, I now choose to courageously dive in and just do it and I deeply and completely love and accept myself.

OCTOBER 9, 2019

HEXAGRAM 57 - INTUITION
Clairaudience.
Intuitive hearing and knowing that helps predict the future
and gives the awareness of when the timing is right to act or organize.

AFFIRMATION:

I trust myself. I trust my intuition. I trust the future.

WRITING ASSIGNMENT:

Please read, respond, and explain your response to each question below.
- What does my intuition feel like?

- How do I receive intuitive awareness?

✸ Make a list of previous events when you trusted your intuition and things worked out well.

-

-

-

-

-

✸ Are there any intuitive hunches you are receiving right now that need attention?

✸ What do you need to do to deepen your intuitive awareness?

✋ EFT SETUP:

Even though it's scary to trust my gut, I now choose to honor my awareness, quiet my mind, and go with what feels right and I deeply and completely love and accept myself.

OCTOBER 13, 2019

21:07:45 GMT

♈ 20 ARIES 14

☾ MOON IN GATE 51.6

The Gate 51 brings us the energy of initiation and sometimes shock.

We are designed to cultivate a relationship with Spirit as part of our direction-given energy. When we fail to take care of our relationship with Spirit we often get "shocked" back onto our path. This gate rules unexpected events and challenges us to stay resilient during times of change and transformation. Reminder, not all unexpected things are bad. Winning the lottery is also a shocking and unexpected event.

 WRITING ASSIGNMENT:

Please read, respond, and explain your response to each question below.
* What needs to be healed, released, aligned, and brought to your awareness for you to stay resilient and to deepen your spiritual connection?

OCTOBER 14, 2019

HEXAGRAM 32 - ENDURANCE
The drive to wait, hold a vision, dream,
and build a foundation for an idea until the time is right.

AFFIRMATION:

My dreams always come true. I would not be given an inspiration without also being given the capacity to realize it into form. I have everything I need to fulfill my dream.

WRITING ASSIGNMENT:

Please read, respond, and explain your response to each question below.
* What would an unlimited life look like to you?

* What would you do?

* What would your business look like?

✳ What new leaps of faith do you need to take?

✳ What new commitments do you need to make?

 **EFT SETUP:**

> Even though I've worked hard to make my dreams come true and nothing has happened yet, I trust in Divine Timing and keep tending to my vision and I deeply and completely love and accept myself.

OCTOBER 20, 2019

HEXAGRAM 50 - VALUES
Nurturing energy that maintains and environment
that supports the sharing of ideas and values.
Teaching, cooking, taking care of.
A Gate of Love.

 AFFIRMATION:

I establish the rules for my reality. I take care and nourish myself so that I may take care and nourish others. Everything I do for others, I do for myself first in order to sustain my energy and power. I rule with self-love and then love freely.

WRITING ASSIGNMENT:

Please read, respond, and explain your response to each question below.
* What new rules do you need to play by?

* Do I need to create new rules in my relationships, my business, for my health, wealth, and welfare?

* Do I love myself?

* Do I need to nurture myself more?

* Do I have the strength and foundation to love freely?

* Do I feel safe in love?

 **EFT SETUP:**

>Even though it's hard for me to give and receive love, I now choose to be completely open to receiving and sharing deep and unconditional love starting first by deeply and completely loving and accepting myself first.

OCTOBER 26, 2019

HEXAGRAM 28 - TENACITY
The ability to fight, endure, and hold on to an idea until it proves it's worth and value. Evolution.

AFFIRMATION:

I am fully alive and I am constantly present to the energy and possibility of Life.

WRITING ASSIGNMENT:

Please read, respond, and explain your response to each question below.
* We often ask ourselves what can we pursue that is worth Dying for? This week, ask yourself: what in your life is worth Living for?

EFT SETUP:

Even though everything feels hard, I now trust that I am mastering what is truly important in my life. I trust the lessons the Universe brings me and I deeply and completely love and accept myself.

OCTOBER 28, 2019

- 03:38:20 GMT
- ♏ 4 SCORPIO 25
- ☾ MOON IN GATE 28.3

The Gate 28 is often called the Gate of Struggle. It can also be called the Gate of Adventure. In its high expression the challenges that present themselves with this gate deepen our awareness of our priorities and what is truly valuable in our lives.

This clarity helps us streamline our creative process and radically prioritize our creative goals. In its low expression, this gate can truly feel like struggle. It's important when this energy is in play to take a long-term view of where you are and your life path right now. Remember that a bump in the road is just a bump.

 WRITING ASSIGNMENT:

Please read, respond, and explain your response to each question below.
- ✻ What are the most important things in your life right now?

- ✻ Is your time, energy, and attention focused on your priorities?

- ✻ What distractions do you need to eliminate?

OCTOBER 31, 2019

HEXAGRAM 44 - PATTERNS

The ability to, with right timing, transmit, or share an idea or tangible good that can help heal the past and create greater value.
The ability to sell an idea.

 AFFIRMATION:

I greet life full on. I move forward confidently into the future knowing that my past has been my greatest teacher. I am not limited but liberated from my past and realize that NOW is the most powerful moment of my life.

WRITING ASSIGNMENT:

Please read, respond, and explain your response to each question below.
* Are there places where I limit myself because of things that have happened to me in the past?

* Am I in full integrity when it comes to leading or influencing others?

* Do I walk my talk?

* Are there places where I need support from others?

Imagine your perception of your life from your deathbed.
* What things would be important to you?

* What accomplishments would you be most proud of?

* Is your life today a good reflection of that perspective?

* Do you need to change your priorities?

EFT SETUP:

Even though it's hard for me to let go of (_____), I deeply and completely love and accept myself.

Even though I am afraid to repeat the past, I now move forward with confidence trusting that I have learned what I needed to learn. I can create whatever future I desire and I deeply and completely love and accept myself.

NOVEMBER 6, 2019

HEXAGRAM 1 - CREATIVITY

The wisdom to recognize that the full expression of your unique potential
IS the creative gift you give the world and the showing the world what that looks like.

 **AFFIRMATION:**

Every day is a new creation. My greatest contribution to the planet is to be the fullest expression of myself as myself. The fulfillment of my Divine Potential is important for the evolution of humanity.

 **WRITING ASSIGNMENT:**

Please read, respond, and explain your response to each question below.
- Are there places where you hold yourself back from fully expressing yourself?

- What will it take for you to step into your fullest expression?

✹ What does the word "legacy" mean to you?

✹ Are you leaving an authentic legacy?

✹ Are there limiting beliefs and experiences you need to release in order to more deeply express your authenticity?

✹ What do you need to do to release these beliefs and experiences?

✋ EFT SETUP:

Even though I am afraid that I am failing my life mission, I now choose to relax and allow my life to unfold before me with ease and grace. I trust that every step I take is perfectly aligned with my soul purpose and I deeply and completely love and accept myself.

NOVEMBER 12, 2019

HEXAGRAM 43 - BREAKTHROUGH
The ability to experience insights into new ideas, thoughts, and inspirations.

 **AFFIRMATION:**

> I take time to enjoy my thoughts. I allow myself to begin to formulate new ideas and inspirations that can create change in my life and in the life of others. I recognize and allow for my own brilliance and serve this brilliance by waiting for the right people to ask me for my insights. My thoughts and ideas are valuable and I trust that what I have to share is valuable to the right people. I attract the right support, circumstances and opportunities that align with my new ideas.

 WRITING ASSIGNMENT:

Please read, respond, and explain your response to each question below.
- ✸ Take some time to "brain dump" all your current thoughts, ideas and inspirations.

* Can you see a pattern of something new emerging?

* Are you on the cusp of a "breakthrough" in your own consciousness or your mindset?

 **EFT SETUP:**

> Even though it's hard to wait for someone to ask me for my insights, I now choose to wait and know that my thoughts are valuable and precious. I only share them with people who value my insights and I deeply and completely love and accept myself.

NOVEMBER 12, 2019

 13:34:16 GMT
 19 TAURUS 52
 MOON IN GATE 23.1 (.2)

The Gate 23 is the gate of explaining and sharing new ideas. This energy supports us in being able to share transformational possibilities and to change the way we think. It's also a great energy that supports us in being able to transmit new ideas to others.

The low expression of this gate can make us struggle with articulating our big new ideas. Sometimes this energy also makes it hard for us to listen. We can miss the cues from others that let us know that the timing is right to share what we know. When we miss these cues, we run the risk of not being heard and missing the chance to help change someone's mind or to transform our own way of thinking.

 ## WRITING ASSIGNMENT:

Please read, respond, and explain your response to each question below.
* What needs to be healed, released, aligned, and brought to your awareness to help you effectively express your unique and transformational ideas?

NOVEMBER 17, 2019

THE 14TH HEXAGRAM - PROSPERITY

The ability to know when to respond to bountiful opportunities. And awareness of which path, experiences, and relationships would produce the greatest wealth and abundance.

 **AFFIRMATION:**

I respond to the things which bring me joy. I pay attention to my excitement and passion and allow myself to trust that the Universe is deliciously conspiring to find ways to support me in the pursuit of my passion. I do what I want to do. I do what feels correct. I honor my joy and excitement and commit to feeling good, knowing that this is the most important contribution I can make to the planet at this time.

 **WRITING ASSIGNMENT:**

Please read, respond, and explain your response to each question below.
* Make a list of everything you are doing right now that you find inspiring and delicious. Make a commitment to yourself to follow at least one of these inspirations each day.

* What would your life look like if you only followed your passion?

* What would you be doing? What would your life feel like?

* What would be your energy level?

* Do you trust the Universe to support you in following your bliss?

* Is it okay to make money doing what you love?

* Can you do what you love and know that you will be supported?

 **EFT SETUP:**

Even though I'm afraid that I can't do what I love and make money, I deeply and completely love and accept myself.

NOVEMBER 23, 2019

HEXAGRAM 34 - POWER

The ability to know when the time is right to act powerfully.
The energy to use power to transform others.
The need to withdraw and integrate before acting with power.

 ### AFFIRMATION:

> I trust the Universe to deliver to me the perfect opportunities to fulfill my dreams and intentions. I watch and wait for signs that clearly show me the next step. I know that my true power is in co-creation with the Universe and I know that Divine Mind has the perfect path for me.

 ### WRITING ASSIGNMENT:

Please read, respond, and explain your response to each question below.
* How are you leveraging your power and energy?

* Are you doing things that are not bringing you closer to your dreams?

✹ What things do you need to stop doing in order to create a space for what you truly want?

✹ What is your definition of power?

✹ Do you feel powerful?

✹ What can you do to be more powerful in your life?

✹ What do you need to do to deepen your trust in the Universe?

✹ Are you showing up and doing your part in your life?

 **EFT SETUP:**

Even though I'm afraid to be powerful, I now choose to fully step into my power and allow the Universe to serve me while I serve it and I deeply and completely love and accept myself.

NOVEMBER 26, 2019

- 15:05:28 GMT
- 4 SAGITTARIUS 03
- MOON IN GATE 34.5

The Gate 34 is the most powerful gate in the Human Design Chart, but there's an irony in this quality of power. It's not the kind of power you can usurp or take. This is power that comes in response to Life and fulfills the needs of the Cosmic Plan.

In its highest expression, it is caring, magnetic, and thoughtful, and leadership.

In its lowest expression, this is inappropriate use of power and the use of power to overpower others. It can also be an unfocused and over-busy way of experiencing life and wasting energy.

This new moon brings us the opportunity for momentum, energy, and expressing ourselves in an empowered way. Use this energy to take guided, bold actions.

 WRITING ASSIGNMENT:

Please read, respond, and explain your response to each question below.
- What do I need to do to fully activate my power?

- How do I feel about being powerful?

- Am I comfortable, safe, and aligned with power?

- And do I trust the universe to show my next right step?

NOVEMBER 28, 2019

HEXAGRAM 9 - FOCUS
The ability to know what to focus on.
The deep dive.

 AFFIRMATION:

I trust the Universe to provide me with everything I need to make my dreams come true. While I wait for the perfect unfoldment of my dreams, I take powerful steps and implement important details to prepare for the manifestation of my intentions. I relax knowing that I am a doing my part in co-creating my life.

WRITING ASSIGNMENT:

- Take a sheet of paper and draw a line down the middle. On top of the left column write the word "Me". On top of the right column write the word "The Universe".
- In the left column make a list of all the things you need to do to make your dream come true. These are the practical 3-D things you need to take care of like write a book, test drive a car, build a website, take a class, etc.
- In the right hand column make a list of all the things the Universe can do. These are the things that may feel beyond your control at the moment, such as attract the perfect clients, friends, or lover, provide the perfect information and the support, etc.
- Doing this exercise will help you discover what concrete, practical baby-steps you can take to make your dreams your reality.

 EFT SETUP:

Even though I've been frustrated with my lack of focus, I now choose to be clear, stay focused and take the actions necessary to create my intentions.

DECEMBER 4, 2019

HEXAGRAM 5 - RHYTHM

The drive and energy for consistency, ritual, and habit.
The ability to harmonize with nature and natural rhythm.

 **AFFIRMATION:**

> I trust and wait. I know that the Universe will reveal the next step to me. I diligently prepare what I know to prepare and I eagerly anticipate what is coming next. I know that Divine Order provides for my abundance and I relax knowing that I'm on my way to creating what I want.

 **WRITING ASSIGNMENT:**

Please read, respond, and explain your response to each question below.
* Are there any last details you need to take care of before you get ready for the next step in your life?

* Is there information you need to master?

✸ Do you need to experiment or explore any new ideas or concepts?

✸ What habits do you need to cultivate or change while you're waiting?

✸ Do you trust the Universe?

✸ Do you need to deepen your trust and connection?

✸ Do you need to cultivate better habits to stay consistent with your connection to Source?

 **EFT SETUP:**

Even though I feel nervous/scared/worried about waiting for Divine Timing, I now choose to create habits that support my connection with Source while I wait and I deeply and completely love and accept myself.

DECEMBER 9, 2019

HEXAGRAM 26 - ACCUMULATION

The ability to transmit ideas and services that help people create more value in their life.
Integrity and Truth.
The ability to "close" a sale and increase value in the world.

 **AFFIRMATION:**

> I speak and act with integrity. My actions and words are in alignment with my intentions. I take my time to speak the perfect words because I know that my words are representations of my heart and my inspirations. I care deeply about my impact and I listen with love to those around me. I take my time and act in alignment with my values and I share my heart freely with my loved ones.

 **WRITING ASSIGNMENT:**

Please read, respond, and explain your response to each question below.
* Are your actions and words in alignment with your intentions?

* What might you need to do to bring them into alignment?

* What truths do you need to share from your heart?

* What heart-to-heart connections do you need to make this week?

* What do you truly value in your life?

* Are you sharing your appreciation?

 **EFT SETUP:**

Even though I am afraid to share my Truth, I now choose to speak my truth clearly and confidently and I deeply and completely love and accept myself.

DECEMBER 12, 2019

05:12:08 GMT
19 GEMINI 52
SUN IN GATE 26
MOON IN GATE 45.4

The Gate 45 is called the Gate of the King or the Queen. Here again, we are exploring the theme of power, set into motion by the new moon.

A good leader leads their people by sharing resources in a generous and equitable way. A leader leads with a deep sense of understanding of their own value and the value of others.

This is leadership that is rooted in service and not personal gain or ego. It is from service that the heart of a leader grows.

This is a powerful time to continue to explore your own sense of self-worth and your willingness to serve the world with your leadership power and skills.

 WRITING ASSIGNMENT:

Please read, respond, and explain your response to each question below.
* What needs to be healed, released, aligned, and brought to your awareness for you to fully activate your leadership and your power?

DECEMBER 15, 2019

HEXAGRAM 11 - IDEAS
The ability to generate multiple possibilities that can lead to new experiences and the fulfillment of new stories and potentials.

❤ AFFIRMATION:

> I honor my inner creative process. I am grateful for every lesson and adventure I have in life and I know that each story of my life experience adds beautiful, rich threads to the tapestry of my own Life Story and the Story of Humanity. I relax and enjoy the quest for Truth in my life, knowing that the more I learn, the more I grow and that the learning and growing never stops. I allow myself to savor every moment and serve as the creative vessel I am. I relax, breathe, trust, and let the ideas flow!

 **WRITING ASSIGNMENT:**

Please read, respond, and explain your response to each question below.
- ✹ Evaluate your achievements and accomplishments of the last few weeks.

- ✹ What ideas do you have to improve what you've done?

- ✹ What did you learn?

- ✹ Keep a running list of ideas this week. You never know when you might find the right person to share them with or when you may hit upon the "million dollar idea" for your life!

    - •

    - •

    - •

    - •

***Remember, the 11 is the Gate of Ideas. You don't have to manifest all of them…or any of them. If an idea is correct for you, it will show up in your life correctly, according to your personal Human Design strategy.

 **EFT SETUP:**

> Even though I've got so many ideas, I now trust that I will know exactly what action to take and when to take it and I deeply and completely love and accept myself.

DECEMBER 20, 2019

HEXAGRAM 10 - SELF-LOVE
The energy to empower others by showing them their love-worthiness.

 **AFFIRMATION:**

I honor that miracle that I am. I am a unique Divine Creation and I know there is no one like me in this world. I make choices and take actions that are honoring of my Divine Magnificence and I surround myself with people who support me, nurture me, inspire me and lift me up. I am powerful and in charge of my Life Direction. I make choices that allow me to fulfill my Divine Potential and in being the fullest expression of myself as myself, I create the space for others to do the same.

 **WRITING ASSIGNMENT:**

Please read, respond, and explain your response to each question below.
* What old energies and "victim stories" do I need to release?

* What does being powerful mean to me?

* What do I need to do to be more empowered?

* Make a list of all the things you love about yourself.
    -
    -
    -
    -

* Write yourself a beautiful love letter and read it out loud to yourself in the mirror.

* What choices and directions could you take that would be in alignment with your self-love?

 **EFT SETUP:**

Even thought it I struggle with loving myself, I now choose to be open to discovering how to love myself anyway and I deeply and completely love and accept myself.

DECEMBER 26, 2019

THE GATE 58 - THE JOY OF LIFE

The energy and the drive to continue to work towards improvement. The deep understanding that joy is in the process not in perfection.

 **AFFIRMATION:**

I am grateful for everything that I am, that I have, and that I have experienced. I allow joy to permeate every cell of my being and I stand in awe of all of my blessings. I relax and know that the shower of blessings that is my life is part of my Divine Heritage and I relax knowing that an endless stream of good flows toward me.

 **WRITING ASSIGNMENT:**

* Make a list of everything you are grateful for. Take a few minutes to really stay in that place of blissful appreciation every day this week.

  •

  •

-
-
-
-
-

✺ More thoughts about THE JOY of LIFE:

 **EFT SETUP:**

Even thought it's hard to let go of the past, I now choose to release it and embrace all the joy that is available to me right now and I deeply and completely love and accept myself.

DECEMBER 26, 2019

 05:13:00 GMT
 4 CAPRICORN 07
 SUN IN GATE 58.1
 EARTH IN GATE 52.1
 MOON IN GATE 58.1

This is the second of two eclipses marking the end of this solar eclipse cycle. We started with the Gate 39, provoking and challenging us to deepen our faith. We end with the Gate 58, called the Joy of Life. This eclipse promises to lighten the energy and intensity of the year. The sun is inviting us to lighten up, to realize that the purpose of all our inner work and personal story re-writing has been to bring us back to a state of mastery of our physical and spiritual world, and into alignment with source and abundance. It is time to relax, honor yourself, and your resiliency. It is time to play.

 WRITING ASSIGNMENT:

Please read, respond, and explain your response to each question below.
    List five fun things you will do before the new year begins.
        1.

2.

3.

4.

5.

✹ What are you most grateful for this year?

✹ What are the biggest lessons you've learned?

JANUARY 1, 2020

HEXAGRAM 38 - FIGHT FOR RIGHT
The energy to know what is truly worth fighting for.

 **AFFIRMATION:**

I have deep clarity about my Life Purpose and direction. Serving my Purpose inspires me and gives me the energy to take powerful steps forward in my life, no matter what comes my way. I am here for a unique purpose and I honor that purpose by setting clear intentions and taking actions that reflect that purpose.

 WRITING ASSIGNMENT:

Please read, respond, and explain your response to each question below.
* What ideas, goals, and visions do I have that are deeply important and vital to me?

* Is there any struggle that is distracting me from knowing what I need to pursue?

* How can I deepen my drive to push towards what is truly valuable and important in my life?

* What do I need to do to clarify my priorities?

 **EFT SETUP:**

Even though things seem hard and challenging, I now choose to use my challenges to help me get clear about what I really want and I deeply and completely love and accept myself.

JANUARY 6, 2020

HEXAGRAM 54 — AMBITION

The Divine Inspiration that inspires a dream or a vision.
The energy to hold that dream or vision until it manifests.

AFFIRMATION:

I am clear. I am focused. I am ready to do whatever it takes to make my dreams come true. I know that my clarity married with my aligned actions are the perfect energies necessary to create miracles in my world. I am noticed, heard, seen, and recognized for what I have to offer and the Universe perfectly conspires with me to make magic happen and my dreams come true.

WRITING ASSIGNMENT:

Please read, respond, and explain your response to each question below.
* What actions do you need to take that will show yourself and the Universe that you are ready for action?

* What steps will you take forward towards your dreams?
  •

-
-
-
-
-

✹ More thoughts about AMBITION:

 **EFT SETUP:**

"Even though I'm afraid my dreams won't come true, I now choose to dream wildly and trust that my dreams will come true. All I have to do is focus my mind, trust, and know that all will unfold perfectly and I deeply and completely love and accept myself."

JANUARY 10, 2020

 19:21:10 GMT
 20 CANCER 00
 SUN IN GATE 54.5
 EARTH IN GATE 53.5
 MOON IN GATE 53.6

This lunar eclipse is the second of two eclipses that set the stage for us to explore our connection with Source and to take our right place in the cosmic unfolding of Life.

This second eclipse in the Gate 53 is the energy of new beginnings. We start the new calendar year with a surge of energy and clarity that pushes us forward into creating what we really want in our lives. This is a vital time for you to get clear about your goals and intentions for the year.

The Gate 53 is the gate of starting things, not necessarily finishing things. The things that are yours to finish are the things that you enter into with faith, and correctly according to your human design strategy. Pay attention and follow the clues to your right next new step.

 WRITING ASSIGNMENT:

Please read, respond, and explain your response to each question below.
* What do you imagine for yourself this year?

✳ What are your dreams, desires, and intentions?

✳ Make a list, keep pictures, or create a video clip to inspire you over the course of the year.

JANUARY 12, 2020

HEXAGRAM 61 - WONDER
The energy to stay in a state of awe and wonder.
The need to contemplate the wonders of the Universe and the world.

AFFIRMATION:

In the stillness I surrender to the Great Mystery of Life and the Divine. I allow Divine Inspiration to wash over me and I listen with great attention and appreciation. I trust that I receive the perfect inspiration and I simply let the inspiration flow to me. I am grateful.

WRITING ASSIGNMENT:

Please read, respond, and explain your response to each question below.
- What do you need to do deepen your connection with Source?

- Do you feel aligned with something bigger than yourself?

* Do you need to create a routine in your daily practice to stay centered and connected?

* More thoughts on WONDER:

 **EFT SETUP:**

> Even though I don't know all the answers, I now choose to surrender and trust that I am being loved, supported, and nurtured by the Infinite Loving Source that is the Universe.

JANUARY 17, 2020

HEXAGRAM 60 - RESOURCEFULNESS
The ability to be inventive with whatever is at hand.
The awareness of what works and the natural ability to focus on and grow what is working.
Optimist.

 **AFFIRMATION:**

I am committed to creating a life that is in alignment with my dreams. I courageously release anything that no longer serves me and I conserve my resources wisely. I know that I am fully supported and that I have been given everything I need to move forward in a powerful way.

 **WRITING ASSIGNMENT:**

Please read, respond, and explain your response to each question below.
- What things might you need to "conserve" for the sake of the future?

- Do you need to change your financial, relationship, health, work, or spiritual habits?

* If so, how?

* Are there any old habits, circumstances, or situations that you need to release to support you in aligning your energy?

* Do you need to improve your focus in order to gain forward momentum?

* If so, what changes in your daily habits do you need to make to improve your focus?

 **EFT SETUP:**

Even though it's hard to let go of things that didn't work, I now release all the clutter from the past and I deeply and completely love, accept and trust myself.

SUMMARY

Your Human Design is your key to understanding your energy, your Life Purpose, your Life Path, and your Soul's Journey in this life time. You are a once-in-a-lifetime cosmic event and the fulfillment of your potential and purpose is the greatest gift you can give the world.

I hope this year has been revolutionary for you and that you re-connected with the True story of Who You Are and the power and possibility of your very special life.

If you need additional support and resources to help you on your life path and soul's journey, please visit www.quantumalignmentsystem.com, where you can find Specialists and Practitioners who will help you understand the story of your Human Design chart, coach you, and help you get to the root of any pain, blocks, or limiting beliefs that may be keeping you from enjoying your Life Story. There are all kinds of free goodies, videos, e-books, and resources to help you on your way!

Thank you again for being YOU! We are who we are because you are who you are!

From my Heart to Yours,
Karen

ABOUT THE AUTHOR

Karen Parker is a #1 best-selling author, Human Design specialist, trainer, professional speaker, and futurist. She has been a high-performance life and business coach for more than 25 years and has coached over 8,000 people. She is deeply dedicated to sharing and co-creating a sustainable, abundant global community.

Karen is the author of:
- *Understanding Human Design the New Science of Astrology: Discover Who You Really Are,*
- *Human Design Activation Guide: Introduction to Your Quantum Blueprint,*
- *Inside the Body of God: 13 Strategies for Thriving in the Quantum World*
- *Abundance by Design: Discover Your Unique Code for Health, Wealth and Happiness With Human Design*
- *The Prosperity Revolution,*
- *EFT for Parents,*
- *Waging Peace in the Face of Rage*

and weekly articles about abundance and spirituality. She is the host of the internationally acclaimed podcast, Quantum Conversations. Karen's work has been featured on Fox News, Bloomberg Businessweek, CBS, ABC, and various radio shows and telesummits.

Karen's website:
www.quantumalignmentsystem.com

Karen is available for private consultations, keynote talks, and to conduct in-house seminars and workshops. You can reach her at Karen@quantumalignmentsystem.com.

www.ingramcontent.com/pod-product-compliance
Lightning Source LLC
Chambersburg PA
CBHW082122230426
43671CB00015B/2780